HOW DO WE PLANT
GODLY CONVICTIONS IN
OUR CHILDREN?

✕CULTIVATING BIBLICAL GODLINESS

Series Editors
Joel R. Beeke and Ryan M. McGraw

Dr. D. Martyn Lloyd-Jones once said that what the church needs to do most of all is "to begin herself to live the Christian life. If she did that, men and women would be crowding into our buildings. They would say, 'What is the secret of this?'" As Christians, one of our greatest needs is for the Spirit of God to cultivate biblical godliness in us in order to put the beauty of Christ on display through us, all to the glory of the triune God. With this goal in mind, this series of booklets treats matters vital to Christian experience at a basic level. Each booklet addresses a specific question in order to inform the mind, warm the affections, and transform the whole person by the Spirit's grace, so that the church may adorn the doctrine of God our Savior in all things.

HOW DO WE PLANT GODLY CONVICTIONS IN **OUR CHILDREN?**

JOEL R. BEEKE

REFORMATION HERITAGE BOOKS
GRAND RAPIDS, MICHIGAN

How Do We Plant Godly Convictions in Our Children?
© 2016 by Joel R. Beeke

Reformation Heritage Books
2965 Leonard St. NE
Grand Rapids, MI 49525
616-977-0889 / Fax 616-285-3246
orders@heritagebooks.org
www.heritagebooks.org

Printed in the United States of America
16 17 18 19 20 21/10 9 8 7 6 5 4 3 2 1

ISBN 978-1-60178-538-1

For additional Reformed literature, request a free book list from Reformation Heritage Books at the above regular or e-mail address.

HOW DO WE PLANT GODLY CONVICTIONS IN **OUR CHILDREN?**

Hear thou, my son, and be wise, and guide thine heart in the way.
—Proverbs 23:19

For years we care for our children like birds care for their nestlings. We shield them from danger, bring them good things to eat, and attend to all their needs. Every father and mother, however, will face the day when their precious children leave the nest and fly on their own. They will no longer abide under our wings and will follow their own beliefs and desires. The whole world will lie before them, and they will make countless choices about work, marriage, children, church, politics, and personal life. While you hope that you will still have a voice in their lives as a trusted counselor and friend, you will never return to the days when you picked up your baby and put him in the pack and play to keep him safe. You will stand at the door and watch him drive away to live his own life.

Therefore, nothing is more essential to the task of bringing children up "in the nurture and admonition of the Lord" (Eph. 6:4) than instilling strong convictions in them. Christian parents should strive to provide each child with an internal biblical compass that will guide him or her through life. Of course, we must recognize our limitations. Our children are not robots that we can program to follow our every directive. Nor should we try to take the place of God, who alone can give our children new hearts and put His Spirit within them so that they willingly do what He commands. Fathers and mothers, however, have a unique opportunity to cultivate in their children the basic convictions by which to navigate their way through life's opportunities and perils. We cannot save them or work faith in them, but we can plant seeds of Bible truth in their hearts and minds that, by God's grace, may bear fruit when they grow to maturity.

The book of Proverbs provides much instruction on how to raise children. Proverbs 23:12 says, "Apply thine heart unto instruction, and thine ears to the words of knowledge." Note that first, Solomon addresses the parents who would teach their children. They must be instructed themselves, seeking "the wisdom that is from above" (James 3:17) and heeding the "words of knowledge" found in God's Word. Note also that from this verse to the end of the chapter, the word "heart" appears no less than seven times. For example, in verse 19 a parent exhorts his child to "hear thou, my son, and be wise, and guide thine heart in the way." Giving heed to parental instruction from the Word of God will make the child "wise unto salvation" (2 Tim. 3:15), enabling him to guide his heart in the way "which leadeth unto life" (Matt. 7:14). Out of the heart flow "the issues of life" (Prov. 4:23).

Tedd Tripp writes:

> This understanding does marvelous things for discipline. It makes the heart the issue, not just the behavior. It focuses correction on deeper things than changed behavior. The point of confrontation is what is occurring in the heart. Your concern is to unmask your child's sin, helping him to understand how it reflects a heart that has strayed. That leads to the cross of Christ. It underscores the need for a Savior. It provides opportunities to show the glories of God, who sent His Son to change hearts and free people enslaved to sin.[1]

The last thing godly parents should want for their children is that they should become little Pharisees, clean on the outside but rotten and dead within. It is important to stress not just their outward behavior but also their consciences, minds, and hearts. We must aim to train the inmost being of our children by informing their minds and shaping their consciences

---

1. Tedd Tripp, *Shepherding a Child's Heart* (Wapwallopen, Pa.: Shepherd Press, 1995), 6.

so that if God's Spirit blesses our children with saving grace, they will live by faith in the Son of God and walk in faithful obedience to God's commands. When our children are little, we may simply tell them what to do. Very early, however, we must also combine enforcement of rules with instruction, and instruction with questions, and questions with conversation. We must see to it that they know what to do, how to do it, and why it matters.

How can we plant godly convictions in our children? The latter part of Proverbs 23 gives us much wisdom about how to do that. I will summarize its teaching in six principles.

PRINCIPLE 1: DISCIPLINE WITH MERCY

Though it may surprise many people today, part of God's loving plan for training young children to direct their hearts with wisdom is to spank them when they need it. Proverbs 23:13–14 says, "Withhold not correction from the child: for if thou beatest him with the rod, he shall not die. Thou shalt beat him with the rod, and shalt deliver his soul from hell." The rod of chastening must be applied not to injure the body and certainly not to give the child what his sins deserve, but only to curb his natural tendency to choose evil and reject good.

Administering corporal discipline is one of the most unpleasant aspects of ruling a household in a godly manner. Some people equate spanking with rage and abuse, but every Christian should remember that "the wrath of man worketh not the righteousness of God" (James 1:20). The rod of wrath is not the rod of correction. Parental discipline must conform itself to the example of our Father in heaven: "Whom the LORD loveth he correcteth; even as a father the son in whom he delighteth" (Prov. 3:12). The motive is love, not anger; the manner is paternal, not judicial; the primary aim is correction, not punishment (see Heb. 12:5–14).

Discipline can go wrong if you don't keep in mind that you are acting in God's stead. Otherwise, the tendency will be to discipline children based on your emotions or personal peeves rather than on God's commands. Unrighteous and self-centered discipline can only provoke children to wrath and diminish you in their regard. If you lose your temper and start yelling, you will soon forget the whole purpose of godly discipline. Never forget that when you discipline, you are disciplining in God's name. He has put the rod of correction in your hand, and you are a steward of that rod on His behalf.

As God's representative, you must administer discipline with the following three characteristics. First, *love*: "My son, despise not the chastening of the LORD; neither be weary of his correction: for whom the LORD loveth he correcteth; even as a father the son in whom he delighteth," says Proverbs 3:11–12. To discipline without love presents your children with the image of Satan, not of God. When Satan afflicts us, his aim is to embitter us against God and so bring about our destruction. When God chastens us, His aim is to make us partakers of His holiness and righteousness (see Heb. 12:10–11).

The second characteristic is *instruction*. Christ says, "As many as I love, I rebuke and chasten: be zealous therefore, and repent…. He that hath an ear, let him hear what the Spirit saith unto the churches" (Rev. 3:19, 22). You must combine rebuke and chastening with an explanation of what your child has done wrong, what repentance looks like, and how free and sure is the grace Christ shows to those who forsake their sins, so that your child's mind and conscience may resonate with the justice and goodness of what you have done. This is one reason why spanking should be applied only when a child is old enough to understand instruction. Take the child into a private room, explain the wrong he has done, and why you need to spank him. Afterward, embrace your child and pray with him. Then regard the matter resolved. Do not bring it up again. As Spurgeon quipped, when you bury a dog, you don't leave its tail sticking up above the ground.

Finally, we must discipline with *compassion*. Psalm 103:13–14 says, "Like as a father pitieth his children, so the LORD pitieth them that fear him. For he knoweth our frame; he remembereth that we are dust." Enter into your child's experience. Recall the power of temptation and the unruliness of the human heart. Identify with him as a sinner who needs to profit from correction. Please note that compassion does not mean foregoing discipline randomly, especially when the child professes repentance immediately. That is a distorted view of divine grace that results in parental inconsistency and can reap hypocrisy in children. But compassion does mean that we limit the discipline to the degree of the moral offense, so that while it must hurt to be effective, it does not harm the child's body or soul. Biblically regulated discipline administered calmly is not child abuse but preventative childcare that can deliver a child from destructive habits and practices.

It might seem that spanking cannot build inner convictions because it applies external force to control a child's behavior, but corporal discipline, lovingly and justly used, helps to form moral and religious convictions. Every child's conscience testifies that there is a God who commands us to do right and forbids us to do wrong and that those who disobey God by doing wrong deserve His punishment (Rom. 1:19–20, 32; 2:14–15). Since the fall of man, however, Satan has beguiled us with his lie that if we sin we "shall not surely die" (Gen. 3:4). Those who believe that lie think their iniquity will not be discovered, and thus they despise and reject the fear of God (Ps. 36:1–2). Sinners "go astray as soon as they be born, speaking lies," says Psalm 58:3, and the most fundamental lie is that sin is good and obedience is bad. Thus, conscience is weakened, blasted, and seared by Satan and sin.

Some parents try to protect their children from the consequences of sin. As a result, their children fail to realize the full import of their bad behavior. Godly parents should apply a judicious measure of pain to teach their children that sin is bad and obedience is good. We know that rebellion against authority, hatred and violence, fornication, stealing, lying, and greed will bring dire consequences upon a child when he becomes an adult and will ultimately send him to hell (1 Cor. 6:9). Children should learn this lesson early in the safety of the home. Corporal discipline, the "rod of correction," greatly helps to strengthen a child's conscience when he is young.

PRINCIPLE 2: REJOICE OPENLY IN WISE CHOICES

If corporal discipline builds negative convictions, then rejoicing and commending children for doing well builds positive convictions. Proverbs 23:15–16 says, "My son, if thine heart be wise, my heart shall rejoice, even mine. Yea, my reins [the seat of emotion in the inward parts] shall rejoice, when thy lips speak right things." If you want to shape your child's heart to delight in doing right, then you must share the rejoicing of your heart in his obedience.

Christian parents may be afraid of praising their children lest it foster pride in them. Parents should learn, however, from the example of the Lord Jesus Christ, who says to His faithful servants, "Well done!... Enter thou into the joy of thy Lord" (Matt. 25:21). Commending a child for doing what is right is a duty that we owe them in the Lord, "for God is not unrighteous to forget your work and labour of love" (Heb. 6:10), and neither should we. Christ taught us that we should find motivation to serve the Lord in the knowledge that the Father knows what we do and will reward us publicly with heavenly treasure (Matt. 6:4, 6, 18–21). A child of God is to live in joyful obedience with a sense of His Father's smile. In the same way, Christian parents should affirm their children with a ready smile, words of praise, and other appropriate rewards when they do well.

This principle is so important that the writer of Proverbs 23 returns to it in verses 24–25: "The father of the righteous shall greatly rejoice: and he that begetteth a wise child shall have joy of him. Thy father and thy mother shall be glad, and she that bare thee shall rejoice." These words are both an encouragement to parents and a guide for their parenting. Some parents may think it wrong to reward obedience, but Scripture declares that in keeping the law of the Lord "there is great reward" (Ps. 19:11). We know that "this reward is not of merit, but of grace" (Heidelberg Catechism, Q. 63); that is, the reward far exceeds the merit of our good works. But we must do as our Father in heaven does! Again, we see how important it is to focus on the heart. As parents, we are not simply trying to control our children's behavior; we are training their hearts to know and do the will of God with delight.

PRINCIPLE 3: INSTILL TRUTH

Proverbs 23:22–23 says, "Hearken unto thy father that begat thee, and despise not thy mother when she is old. Buy the truth, and sell it not; also wisdom, and instruction, and understanding." Solomon borrows imagery from the marketplace: parents are selling wares to their children. He urges the parents to market precious commodities to their children—words of truth, wisdom, instruction, and understanding. He urges their children to buy up all they can and hold on to it for dear life. In other words, parents— especially fathers, who are called to be teaching "prophets" in their home—must teach truth to their children so that they will grow in understanding and, by God's grace, in wisdom. Here are several helps for fathers to be prophetic teachers and truth instillers for their children.

Teach as God's Authorized Steward
Part of our earnestness in instilling truth in our children comes from knowing that God has commanded us to teach them. Ephesians 6:4 says, "Fathers, provoke not your children to wrath: but bring them up in the nurture and admonition of the Lord." We say to them, "Children, God gave me this task of teaching you. I must follow His command." Churches and Christian schools may supplement our efforts, but the primary responsibility of teaching covenant children belongs to parents, especially to fathers. They

should not delegate all the responsibility to other teachers and consider their own job done.

Teach through Family Worship

Daily family worship ought to be the basic context for the exercise of your prophetic office toward your children. Teach your children "all the counsel of God," as Paul says he did for the Ephesians (Acts 20:27). Your home should be a little church or seminary in which you are to serve as a prophet, teaching your children God's precious truth—addressing the mind, the conscience, the heart, and the will of each of them. Teach your children Bible stories and doctrines, applying those stories and doctrines to their daily lives for their proper spiritual, moral, and psychological development.

Using a guide such as the *Reformation Heritage KJV Study Bible*,[2] teach your children about each book of the Bible, showing them its major theme and how it leads us as needy sinners to Jesus Christ. Teach them the main points in each chapter you read. You can ask them questions and discuss the passage you just read. Help them memorize the Ten Commandments, the Lord's Prayer, and the Apostles' Creed. Describe who God is and what He is

---

2. The *Reformation Heritage KJV Study Bible* (Grand Rapids: Reformation Heritage Books, 2015) features a "Thoughts for Family Worship" section at the end of each chapter to provoke conversation and encourage better understanding of the passage.

like. Teach them the origin, pervasiveness, and consequences of sin. Teach them the necessity of the
new birth and of personal repentance and faith in
Christ alone for salvation. Teach them about the aton-
ing blood of Christ and its efficacious power. Present
the whole Christ to your children: His person and
natures, His offices and states, and His beauty and all-
sufficiency. Teach them about the moral law and its
civil, evangelical, and didactic uses. Teach them
about God's call to holiness and how to live a life of
thankfulness. Set before them the reality of death,
the solemnity of judgment, the joy of heaven, the tor-
ments of hell, and the timelessness of eternity.

As you teach, be plain in meaning and style.
Be simple and short. Be experiential and relevant
in application. Be affectionate in manner, like the
father in Proverbs. Reach down into the life of your
children by using age-appropriate illustrations and
concrete concepts. Review and simplify sermons
you've heard as a family in church. Tether biblical
instruction to current events in your family, society,
and nation as much as possible.

Teach by Example
In addition to being our chief prophet, Jesus is the
living Word (John 1:1, 14). He revealed God not only
in His words but also in His life. Be like Paul, who
advised Timothy, his dear son in the Lord, "But thou
hast fully known my doctrine, manner of life, purpose,
faith, longsuffering, charity, patience, persecutions,

afflictions…what persecutions I endured: but out of them all the Lord delivered me" (2 Tim. 3:10–11). We are always teaching our children, whether we know it or not, for they are reading the book of our lives. Besides the Bible, our lives are the most important book our children will ever read. In the book of our life, they will see how important our views on God are, whether worship is a delight or a duty, whether sin is a horrible evil or mere naughtiness, and whether we really cherish our families or view them as a burden.

Teach by Sharing Your Life
Paul openly spoke about his problems, afflictions, and weaknesses. He boasted in his weaknesses so that others could see the power of Christ in him and the sufficiency of God's grace in all his trials (2 Cor. 12:9–10). He opened his life to others so that they would open their lives to him (2 Cor. 6:11–13). Happy are the children who can say to their friends, "My mom and dad are pretty neat; I can talk to them about anything." That does not mean you function as their buddy, for that would negate your authority over them as a Christian parent. But it does mean you should strive to become their confidant in a friendship that deepens as they mature. Jesus called His disciples "friends" because He loved them enough to die for them and to share with them the whole counsel of God (John 15:13–15).

Teach for Holistic Maturity

Luke 2:52 tells us that "Jesus increased in wisdom and stature, and in favour with God and man." Christ is our model of child development; He was born a baby but grew into an adult in all aspects of His humanity.

In addition to training your children's minds and hearts so that, by God's grace, they grow and mature in serving God, train them also in social graces. A well-trained mind unaccompanied by basic good manners or courtesy is a blunt sword. Our children should show respect to older people, kindness to their peers, and compassion to persons younger than they are. If you expect your children to behave well but do not teach them proper etiquette, you set them up for failure in society. Furthermore, give them opportunities to enjoy fine art, great literature, and good music as gifts of God's common grace. That too will mature them and enhance their lives.

Train your children physically as well. Teach them that their bodies are gifts from God, so they must respect the rules of health. They need a certain amount of sleep, a healthy diet, and plenty of exercise. Teach your children the facts of life, discussing openly the goodness, spiritual significance, and God-given boundaries of their sexuality. Do not leave that education to their peers. Guide them in matters of personal appearance so that they dress modestly and attractively but not to draw attention to themselves.

Teach with Passion

We have heard some preachers proclaim God's word in a rather cold, mechanical manner. Consider by contrast the prophet Jeremiah's zeal: "His word was in mine heart as a burning fire shut up in my bones, and I was weary with forbearing, and I could not stay" (Jer. 20:9). The prophet could not keep God's word in; he had to speak it.

Likewise, Amos felt compelled to speak when God told him to do so. He said, "The lion hath roared.... The Lord GOD hath spoken, who can but prophesy?" (Amos 3:8). Many times my dad wept as he taught us the truths of God. That was passionate teaching. My father was bringing us the word of God not as dry, boring information, but as the living Word, "powerful, and sharper than any twoedged sword" (Heb. 4:12), to instill truth in us. He would often say to us when imparting truth, "I wish I could write this with an iron pen on your heart"—and with the Spirit's help he did! Likewise, we must teach our children with passion.

PRINCIPLE 4: DIRECT CHILDREN TO FEAR AND HOPE IN THE LORD

For your children to develop enduring convictions, they must learn to look beyond you to the Lord. The father counsels his son in Proverbs 23:17–18, "Let not thine heart envy sinners: but be thou in the fear of the LORD all the day long. For surely there is an end; and thine expectation shall not be cut off." The problem here is the temptation to "envy sinners." Wicked men seem to prosper in this world, but not for long; their expectation shall be cut off by the cold hand of death (Ps. 49:11, 17–20). Children see what other kids are allowed to do, and they may resent not having the same freedom. Envy can arise in their hearts, even in the godly, who are tempted to say, "Verily I have cleansed my heart in vain" (Ps. 73:13).

God urges parents to move beyond "because I said so" and direct their children to the Lord as the reason for obedience. Proverbs 23:17–18 joins together fear of the Lord and hope in the Lord: "Be thou in the fear of the LORD.... Thine expectation shall not be cut off." Fear of God and hope in God are two aspects of saving faith. On the one hand, we must communicate to our children the majestic and moral holiness of God so they will fear Him and turn away from evil. We must speak often of His righteous judgment against sin and the dire consequences of persevering in it. On the other hand, we must teach them the faithfulness and lovingkindness of God so they hope in His word and persevere in doing what is right in His sight. We must teach them God's promises, such as Psalm 33:18, "Behold, the eye of the LORD is upon them that fear him, upon them that hope in his mercy," and Psalm 147:11, "The LORD taketh pleasure in them that fear him, in those that hope in his mercy."

Though our children are young and naïve, they have souls and may ask deep questions. They want to know why we must do some things and avoid others. Granted, they must submit to our authority because God commands them to honor us. Our parenting should consistently direct our children beyond ourselves, however, to our great and good God. Lasting spiritual and moral convictions can be grounded only in the knowledge of God. The beauty of this approach is that it opens the way for us to share the gospel of Jesus Christ.

Fear of God and hope in God are core convictions to instill in your children, so let me develop this point in more detail. Three aspects of cultivating this godly fear and firm hope in our children may be summarized in the words *confession*, *communion*, and *consecration*.

Confession of Sin

For sinners, who are fallen in Adam, the fear of the Lord cannot be separated from the confession of sin. Proverbs 28:13–14 says, "He that covereth his sins shall not prosper: but whoso confesseth and forsaketh them shall have mercy. Happy is the man that feareth alway: but he that hardeneth his heart shall fall into mischief [calamity]." In confessing sin, we acknowledge that we have sinned in failing to do what God commands and by doing what God forbids; therefore we deserve His wrath and punishment. At the same time, according to God's promises, we may also look to His mercy in Christ for forgiveness (Ps. 130:3–5).

A powerful way to teach our children to confess their sins is to confess our sins to them. I am not advising you to tell your children all your sins, but to confess any sins that are part of your dealings with them. For example, if you involve your children in your sin, whether it is gossip, idle talk, covetousness, or envy, it is important to lead them out of that sin by being the first to repent. Likewise, if you sin against your children, go quickly to make amends. When you parent wrongly, you need to say to your child, "I did this and it was wrong. Will you forgive me?" Identify your sin to them in biblical terms so that they can see which commandment you have transgressed.

When my son was about three years old, I had to take him into the room where we disciplined our children. We talked, prayed, and spanked, and then we prayed, kissed, and hugged. We walked out of the room holding hands, and I'll never forget how he looked me in the face and said, "Daddy, how come you never sin?" I was astonished and went back in the room with him and said, "Son, I want you to understand, I'm a big sinner. I'm needy just like you. There's only one who doesn't sin, and that's Jesus. I've done many wrong things in my life. I need the Savior every moment, for I'm a sinner just like you." Our children need to hear that from our lips.

We must also train our children to confess their sins. We cannot let children get away with known sin without confession. Some time ago at our seminary conference, a child noticed that we had candy set out in dishes between the sessions. Later, his parents discovered that he had helped himself without their permission, filling his pockets with no less than sixty pieces of candy. The father looked him straight in the eye and said, "Tomorrow, you must hand this bag of candy back to Dr. Beeke and confess your sin." The child turned white and said, "No, I can't do that!" and began to cry. He was very upset, but the parents stood their ground. In the morning, the boy came to his father and said, "Dad, I'm feeling better now." His father asked him what had happened, and he said, "Last night I confessed my sin to God, and He forgave me, and I thought if a holy God will forgive me, maybe Dr. Beeke will forgive me too."

The parents brought the child to me and said they were open to whatever punishment I thought was appropriate. After hearing his confession, I forgave the boy and hugged him. A bit later, he came back, sat beside me, chatting away about how he might want to serve the Lord as a pastor someday. Dear friends, do not neglect to teach your children to confess their sins and make things right with those they have sinned against. Confession and forgiveness are sweet experiences of grace and crucial exercises to develop the graces of fear of God and hope in God.

Communion with God
Fear of God and hope in God flourish in the awareness that we always live under His watchful eyes.

Proverbs 15:3 says, "The eyes of the LORD are in every place, beholding the evil and the good." The "eyes" of God represent not merely His knowledge but His active presence to bless or to chasten according to His covenant (2 Chron. 16:9; Prov. 5:21). We constantly stand *coram Deo* (before the face of God). R. C. Sproul says, "To live *coram Deo* is to live one's entire life in the presence of God, under the authority of God, to the glory of God."[3] When the Lord called Abraham, He said, "I am the Almighty God; walk before me [in my presence, literally, to my face], and be thou perfect" (Gen. 17:1). By training our children to acknowledge God's presence everywhere, we lay a foundation for a lifetime of walking in fellowship "with the Father, and with his Son Jesus Christ" (1 John 1:3).

Urge your children to live with the consciousness that God is ever present, always watching. That will keep them from sin and encourage them to seek the Lord's blessing and to do His will. They will learn to live on praying ground, knowing to pray spontaneously over everything, whether they cry out in need or thank God for His goodness.

Two young girls got some cookies from their mother to take to Grandma. The last thing their mother said was, "Make sure you don't open the box and take one along the way. They're all for Grandma."

---

3. R. C. Sproul, *In the Presence of God: Devotional Readings on the Attributes of God* (Nashville: Thomas Nelson, 1999), xii.

Along the way, one of them said, "What if we just took one cookie? No one's looking." She set the box down and lifted off the cover.

The other girl said, "Wait a minute! Someone's looking!"

The first girl was startled, and said, "Who?"

Her sister said, "*God* is looking." That's the conviction you want to build in your children.

God's presence should not just threaten your children; it should also comfort them in Christ by the Spirit. David rejoices in the thought that wherever he might go, even down to "the uttermost parts of the sea," he knew that "thou art there" (Ps. 139:9, 8, respectively). I remember the day my dad took me into his bedroom and said, "Son, there's something I want to teach you, and I hope you never forget it. If you're a child of God, you always have a place to go—to the triune God, no matter what happens in your life." That teaching has been precious to me, especially when I have gone through trials in life.

More specifically, how should we teach our children about Trinitarian communion with God? We should teach our children to look to the Father as the head of God's family by honoring His laws wherever they go. We should teach them that there is no communion with God apart from the blood of Jesus Christ that "cleanseth us from all sin" (1 John 1:7). As sinners, we are far from God, but God brings us near "by the blood of Christ. For he is our peace" (Eph. 2:13–14). Therefore, when you teach your children that they live in the presence of God, stress that Christ "was delivered for our offences, and was raised again for our justification" (Rom. 4:25). We should teach them to exercise faith in Christ for everything they need in the Christian life—from repentance, to obedience, to assurance—and bathing all these in continual and habitual prayer. Only by faith in Jesus Christ our guilt is removed, our hearts are renewed, and our lives are blessed by God. We should teach them to trust in the Spirit by praying that He would bless them in reading the Bible and in bringing Scripture to their minds throughout the day so that they would live to the Father through faith in Christ. Teach this kind of Trinitarian comfort to yourself as well, for you cannot train your children to live in communion with the triune God if you are a stranger to Him.

Consecration to the Glory of God

To fear the Lord is to acknowledge Him as God, to serve Him as Lord, and to honor Him as Father. The opposite of fearing God is not ignoring Him but despising Him (Prov. 14:2). Therefore, it is important to show your children that communion with God is necessary in order to live *soli Deo gloria* (to the glory of God alone). Our children must be taught that "the chief end of man is to glorify God, and to enjoy Him forever" (Westminster Shorter Catechism, Q. 1). If we can instill this truth in our children, many other convictions will fall into place for them. Our children will then know how to respond when their friends tempt them to sin through peer pressure. They will know what they should do when they sin against a friend or neighbor. Hopefully, they will not dare to be part of anything that does not bring glory to God.

God's glory must trump all other considerations, including personal and family honor. Christians must not become family-centered in an idolatrous manner. Teach your children that life is more about God than about self or family. You want to build a close family, but you don't want to build a family that is its own be-all and end-all. Live in such a way that everything in personal and family life revolves around the glory of God. Teach your children that your family is just one of many families serving God around the globe, and they all exist for the honor of our Lord.

A God-fearing teenage son sent his father a note about a major event coming in his life. He wrote, "Dad, if the Lord gives this to me I'll praise Him, and if He doesn't give it to me I'll praise Him, because He gets the glory for everything." What joy those words brought to the father's heart! Ultimately, what happens to us on earth doesn't matter that much, for we are headed for eternity, and the glory of the Lord will be our reward.

Dear parents, do whatever you can to teach your children to fear God and to hope in His word. Show them by your example the basic practices of the Christian life: confession of sin, communion with God, and consecration to His glory. These convictions will lead to stability and happiness. Indeed, these are the foundations of all other true convictions. There is no greater blessing than to fear God, for the smiles and frowns of God are of greater weight than the smiles and frowns of mere human beings. Proverbs 14:26–27 says, "In the fear of the LORD is strong confidence: and his children shall have a place of refuge. The fear of the LORD is a fountain of life, to depart from the snares of death."

PRINCIPLE 5: WARN AGAINST DESTRUCTIVE LIFESTYLES

Another way to build convictions in your children is to warn them against patterns of sin that particularly threaten young people. Proverbs 23 presents three examples of these lifestyles.

Self-Indulgent Lifestyle

First, warn them against a self-indulgent lifestyle. Against the mind-set that says, "We just want to have fun," Proverbs 23:20–21 admonishes us, "Be not among winebibbers; among riotous eaters of flesh: for the drunkard and the glutton shall come to poverty: and drowsiness shall clothe a man with rags." Notice how the wise father speaks openly about specific sins and warns against wasting money to gratify the appetites of the body and the poverty that results from failing to get out of bed and go to work.

A self-indulgent lifestyle may take many forms. In today's American culture, it often manifests itself in an obsession with electronic communications and entertainment. Many children waste away hours in front of a screen watching movies, playing video games, or using various apps to send messages and share media. Please don't think I am against electronic devices or media used as tools. The problem arises when our goal is no longer to serve and glorify God, and we settle in to "amuse ourselves to death," as one writer put it. Instead of being diligent in school and at work and building real friendships, our children risk being caught in a web of superficial connections and virtual reality. As a result, many teenagers suffer from depression, isolation, and loneliness and are vulnerable to manipulation by those who control the media they are addicted to.

So much of the Christian life is about learning to do the right things, at the right times, and in the right way. There is a time to play as well as a time to work. The real difficulty of the Christian life is learning to take hold of every facet of life and to channel it self-consciously to God's glory in light of Scripture.

We need to warn our children of the danger of living to please themselves and failing to discipline themselves. We must teach them the deeper pleasures of hard work and service to others. Work is not just something that we have to do, although the principle still holds "that if any would not work, neither should he eat" (2 Thess. 3:10). Rather, we should teach them that work is a calling from God and a delight for those created in the image of God (Gen. 1:26–28). We don't need to rail against popular activities, but we should ask our children, "Is this the best use of your time?" Young people generally do not appreciate how precious time is and how it cannot be regained when it is gone.

Sexually Immoral Lifestyle

Warn them against a sexually immoral lifestyle. This lifestyle is driven by the mind-set that sex is the ultimate human experience. Proverbs 23:27–28 says, "A whore is a deep ditch; and a strange woman [strange because she is not your wife] is a narrow pit. She also lieth in wait as for a prey, and increaseth the transgressors among men." Here again we see the wise father admonishing his son by naming a particular sin and speaking of its horrible consequences. The images of a "deep ditch" and "narrow pit" communicate how sexual immorality kills people, body and soul, and how difficult it is to escape this trap once you fall into it. We must teach our children not to see those who would seduce them as people who care about them but as robbers who will steal what is precious and then leave them humiliated, shamed, or even dead. Despite all the language of love that is used to describe immorality, in reality it makes people into transgressors who act treacherously and betray those to whom they should be faithful.

Substance-Abuse Lifestyle

Warn them against a substance-abuse lifestyle. The mind-set of this lifestyle is, "I need alcohol or drugs to be happy." Proverbs 23:29–35 offers a vivid depiction of substance (alcohol) addiction, beginning with the questions, "Who hath woe? who hath sorrow?" then describing the evils of addiction, and ending with the pathetic wish of the addict, "I will seek it yet again." Given that alcohol or drugs are often a gateway to social acceptance for young people, our children must be taught how mind-altering substances destroy friendships, promote contention, incite violence, and impair the body (v. 29), determine our social lives (v. 30), enslave the senses (v. 31), bring pain and death (v. 32), corrupt our minds and speech (v. 33), cause us to lose control of our bodies and thoughts (v. 34), numb our healthy sense of pain so that we do not know when we are in grave danger (v. 35), and make us willing slaves (v. 35).

Some sins call for special warnings. All sins have the spark of hell within them and can ignite a person's whole life, resulting in eternal damnation. Certain sins, however, have the tendency to seize a naïve young person with the deadly force of a pit bull terrier. Fathers, learn from the advice of the wise father of Proverbs. Warn your children against lifestyles that may appear attractive but will only lead them to death. Teach them how to have fun in a way that is good for their bodies, minds, and souls and helps them develop healthy relationships with other people.

PRINCIPLE 6: SET A TRUSTWORTHY EXAMPLE

In warning his children against destructive lifestyles, the wise father calls his child to trust him and to observe his own lifestyle. Proverbs 23:26 says, "My son, give me thine heart, and let thine eyes observe my ways." "Give me thine heart" means, "Trust me to guide you" (see v. 22). That implies openness (2 Cor. 6:11–13) not just to a father's teachings but also to his "ways" or conduct. The father asks his son to watch how his father lives and to follow him in the same path of obedience.

Regardless of how old your children are or how mature they appear to be, you must model for them a life of deep convictions. If our children see that we take biblical truths lightly, that will influence them to take our teaching lightly. You can't teach your children what you yourself don't value.

A striking example of this is Luke's account of the Lord's Prayer. In Luke 11, we are told that Jesus "was praying in a certain place, [and] when he ceased, one of his disciples said unto him, Lord, teach us to pray" (v. 1). Jesus first practiced before them what He then taught them as His model prayer. It was His example that opened their hearts to His instruction. In the three and a half years the disciples traveled with Jesus, He showed them that prayer was a necessary discipline for a godly life.

In a similar way, we need to model our convictions for our children. They need to see us in
communion with God. They need to see us reading
and studying the Scriptures and sound Christian literature. They need to see us bless others with our
confession of faith as well as by our efforts to help
the downtrodden, widowed, and orphaned. They
need to see how much we love Jesus Christ and
His church.

Consider how you can model prayer for your
children. Begin in your private prayers and devo-
tions each day. In family worship, pray with and for
your children. But do not end there. Make prayer
both sides of the coin of your life. James 5:13 says, "Is
any among you afflicted? let him pray. Is any merry?
Let him sing psalms." So let every sorrow or need
stir you to petition and every joy and blessing move
you to praise. Children need to see in our lives that
prayer is the most natural, habitual, spontaneous,
and important ingredient.

How does that work out in practice? Imagine
that you are on family vacation and you drive by
a serious car accident. You see the ambulances and
drive on because the people are being taken care of.
But you can also help by praying. It should be natural for your children to hear you say as a parent,
"Children, let's pray now for the family that was in
that accident."

Or imagine that you have gotten your teenage
daughter a cell phone because she is driving and

will need it for her safety. Do you just hand it to her? No, you say to her, "Here is your cell phone. This can be an instrument for much good or great harm. I want you to take it to your bedroom, lay it on the bed, get down on your knees, and pray to God that you'll never use that cell phone for an evil purpose but only for the glory of God."

Or imagine that someone shares a need or concern, and you say, "I will pray for you." Why not pray with that person right then? If necessary, you can step into a semiprivate setting so as not to disrupt what is going on. Your children should grow up seeing you "pray without ceasing" (1 Thess. 5:17).

Paul wrote in 1 Timothy 4:4–5, "For every creature of God is good, and nothing to be refused, if it be received with thanksgiving: for it is sanctified by the word of God and prayer." Take everything that God gives you and sanctify it with prayer. That is a way to offer ourselves up to God day by day as a living sacrifice for His glory.

Fathers and mothers, think of your faith in Christ and your attitude toward life as a fragrance or aroma. What aroma permeates your home and your workplace? Just as your whole house will take on the predominant aroma of what is done in it, such as baking bread, your children will tend to absorb the fragrance of your life. What are they getting from you? Love? Hope? Joy? Patience? Purity? Praise? Or the bitter stench of anger, bitterness, unbelief, and sin? "Do as I say and not as I do" is a sure formula for disaster in parenting.

Ultimately, Christ Himself is the pattern for all godly living. Even the best father cannot measure up to this height. We can show our children how to repent and how to pray and a host of other exemplary matters, but Christ alone can show them the full scope of Christian character in glorious perfection.

CONCLUSION: BUILD CONVICTIONS AT DIFFERENT STAGES OF LIFE

Six principles from Proverbs 23 direct us how to plant convictions in our children for Christ's glory and their good: Discipline them with love. Rejoice openly in their wise choices. Instill truth in them. Direct them to fear the Lord and hope in His word. Warn against destructive lifestyles. Set a trustworthy example. Our children can turn to those principles for guidance for the rest of their lives and, like Caleb, follow God fully all their days (Num. 14:24).

Children go through different stages of life, and your planting convictions in them should reflect this development. The first stage is *regulation*. This is the time governed almost entirely by rules. When our children are very young, it is important that parents regulate what they do. They don't need to be stern authoritarians. But since young children often lack discernment, they need clearly drawn lines as to what is right and wrong. It is our duty as parents to guide our children in this stage with a clear yes or no. The rules must be enforced. When our children disobey, we must discipline them and restore them to the path of obedience.

The second stage is *participation*. As children get older, they increasingly need to know the reasons for these rules and how they apply. Parents should then emphasize the principles of biblical and Christ-centered morality and wisdom. As children grow, their parents should invite them to participate in the process of making decisions by applying biblical principles to specific situations. It's like taking the grammar they learned in elementary school and using it to write a book report, or taking arithmetic and using it to solve a real-life problem in household finances.

For instance, your child comes to you and says, "Dad, I'm really interested in watching this movie with my friend. May I?" Instead of simply saying no, take the opportunity to build on the rules you have instilled in him. Ask questions like, Why do you want to watch this movie? Do you believe it will be edifying? Can you glorify God more by watching it than not? Can you ask God's blessing on what you are hoping to do? Teach your children at this stage how to assess the situation, their own hearts, the circumstances, and the subject. Help them think through their decisions. At some point you still need to make the final decision.

The third stage is *integration*. This is the time when our children are older and increasingly able to make their own decisions, which will help them later when they move out and begin to live independently. At this point they are still evaluating what they have learned and experienced and determining their own views. As long as they live in your home, you have the right to expect them to live by the rules of your household. They should be making more and more choices on their own, however, especially when they become legal adults.

In this stage of development, you can still offer advice. If you don't think it is wise for your son to spend money and time traveling to the Bahamas for spring break with his college friends, share your concerns. By this time, Lord willing, your son knows that your aim is not to control his life but to help him along in life's journey. You are not trying to keep him as a young bird in the nest for all his days. Rather, you are hoping he will soon fly with the wings of an eagle in a Christward direction.

The final stage is *supplication.* When children become adults, get married, and leave your home to establish their own families, you may no longer instruct or advise as you could previously. If they ask your advice, you should feel free to give it. Nevertheless, you must be careful not to infringe upon the new family unit. The time has come when we should talk more to our God about our children than we do to our children about our God. We petition—yes, we supplicate and intercede at the mercy seat of heaven—that the triune God may bless all the efforts we have made, for Christ's sake, to build convictions into our children and that He may lead all of them by His Word and Spirit to the celestial city to be married with Christ forever. What parent can send up enough petitions to God's merciful throne for their adult children (whether married or single) and their grandchildren?

In all the stages our children go through, we parents are called to be conviction planters in what we say and do, always pointing them to the name of Jesus, for "there is none other name under heaven given among men, whereby we must be saved" (Acts 4:12). Do not overestimate or underestimate your influence. You cannot control your children, nor can you save them. You are not responsible for what they choose to do as adults. However, you can sow good seed in the soil of their hearts year after year, and by God's grace that seed will bear much good fruit. May God grant this fruition in your family, in the families that your children raise, and in every generation that follows until our Lord returns, for the sake of His own Son, His own covenant, and His own glory.